T0151664

Swallows and Waves

Paula Bohince

Sarabande Books
Louisville, Kentucky

FIRST EDITION

Library of Congress Cataloging-in-Publication Data

Bohince, Paula, 1976–
 [Poems. Selections]
Swallows and waves : poems / Paula Bohince. — First edition.
    pages ; cm
 ISBN 978-1-941411-15-5 (softcover) — ISBN 978-1-941411-16-2 (ebook)
I. Title.
PS3602.O443A6 2016
811'.6—dc23

                              2015017011

Cover by Denny Schmickle
Interior by Sarabande Books
Manufactured in Canada.
This book is printed on acid-free paper.
Sarabande Books is a nonprofit literary organization.

 The Kentucky Arts Council, the state arts agency, supports
Sarabande Books with state tax dollars and federal funding from
the National Endowment for the Arts.

Poems in this collection are based on scroll paintings and woodblock prints from Japan's Edo period, which spanned 1603–1868.

For Patrick

Contents

A Woman Coming from under the Mosquito Netting and Lighting Her Pipe at the Wick of a Lantern

Shawled in loose waves of blue,

sprawled barefoot before the flame, the un–

done day collapses, looks at itself

as into a mirror, clarifying the bad dog

who frightened her walk.

In reflection, that disturbance

quells, and she lies large on ankles,

hair up: the last formality. Otherwise lax

as sensation caught in a thought-sea.

Rooster and Hen before Hydrangeas

Drenched azure, bunched and hung. Sea-
grapes poised to become sea-wine,
vinegar if love is unrequited. Trellis to shade
both *coq* and *coquette,*
his tail a fury of feathers, waterfall-white.
Red comb curled forward, glinting threat
of golden spur, he will tame her,
though she hides behind fans of wings,
kimono sleeves of wings.
The question posed, now all between them is
a test, *pas de deux* of sense and patience.

Lover Taking Leave of a Courtesan

He stands and dresses
but slowly, to show reluctance.
This is dawn's performance.
She from the spent cushion
grasps his clothing, not
to keep him but to indicate pleasure-
given loyalty.
Fuji is present, as a painted
screen. The real exists, hidden
behind it. The man,
woman are representatives
also, though the pain, the nature
of pain, is personal.

Hibiscus and Korean Nightingale

Night's neglect is a gift. Images erase. Bitter-
sweet longing becomes inflected
with song. But it is daylight. He's alone against
the noiseless hibiscus, the horizon's haze, an ache in his
throat. The spell has worn off.
When speech elevates to music, certain honesties
are gilded over. The stilled gold bell
of his lovely body rang and rang, until wrung. Sang to
an *anyone* until dawn, and she didn't come.

Tiger Licking Its Leg

Three-petaled pink of tongue. Un-kissed
perhaps since cubhood,
mother long wandered, the mouth asserts calm
assurances all over the chaotic body.
On high rocks, fierceness softens, as Heaven
reverses Earth's sins.
Furred as a bee, striations of stripes like rivers
forking nowhere. Pupils widen
in pleasure. In the hot dawn, its whiskers,
curling tail, those danger-sensors, are put on
low-alert, in this the new day's caress.

Hairdresser

Seated one, loved by the lavishing comb
and fingers of another woman demon-
strating how attention and technique coalesce
into art. Where to go
when the mother is gone.
All occupations form to replace her.
What relief to be a girl again for an hour,
beneath the practiced wrists of her avatar.

Tiger and Dragon

The more mythic one un-scrolled: fantasy

above sea spray. Fright in the eyes of the Emperor.

Also fight, talons drawn. He flies

in the smoke of his dying, bare earth unlocking

by seconds into spirit.

The tiger, by contrast, is relaxed on land, calm

and sensuous as a woman

dreaming beneath strange embroidery, whose death

is distant. Whose beauty is armor, again.

Two Women, One Seated on a Bench Smoking a Pipe and Another Holding a Fan, under the Light of the Crescent Moon

The one who smokes has bared her breasts,

exposed them to the drowsy

eye, her companion. Glowing, the crescent

undersides are sated smiles. Rebellious

nipples relax.

The friend stays dressed,

but her *obi* has loosened, the common

sandal suggests a similar mood. As the moon

is one thing and many: shy to bold.

Some nights grows faint, fan-like, and folds.

Sparrows and Camellia

With thimble weight, the sparrows alight

on decorative branches.

Thumbs on a slightly bored body

twiddling the thinnest edges. The day's

assignment: to while the afternoon

away. Maintain the blurred

between. It is easy

as friendship between love affairs,

vacant of extremity, passion. How cool

the light in this region of no awe. Welcome

middle register: sane, calm.

Riverboat Party

A boatman reclines on the roof

and smokes. In mist, he is invisible,

swept along, an absent–

minded god. The party below plays

Go. Absorbed in the game,

given no cause to contemplate,

they don't. What the river,

if made of hours and minutes instead

of water and fish means, finally.

An Eagle Attacking a Monkey under a Pine Tree

The eagle, white as terror, is the narrow

world now. The monkey, its cushiony dream of this

other world, is nearly done. Painful,

it will be painful to the end. Then what is asked for

is not survival but quickness.

Another monkey, high in the pine, must witness.

While holding a rock that will not release.

One must think *It would be no use,* then sit up to Nature

and give thanks to that schoolmistress.

Girl Playing Samisen

Plucking the triplet strings, reading solemnly
the music on her lap, she struggles
to leave behind her body, become a vibrating instrument,
quiver of song. The caged
bird over her shoulder listens: solo audience.
Its notes once called forth a mate, or answered a request.
Now the marriage is between itself and the girl
who will be one day a true wife, wanting to learn before
then the lonely joy of the samisen.

Peacock

Aloft above the pale

and more robust chrysanthemums,

observing his own wake

of plumage, gazing toward

the absent spouse, his glory is

behind him. Kingly

in robes that grow each year

heavier, his pact is with grandeur.

Even in loss, it is his,

this cascade of feathers without

cause to flourish anymore.

Sudden Rain on Mt. Tempō

Coarse clouds, black as gunpowder, release their
ammunition, slashing in one direction
the bowed sail, the prow, the deck of the mighty ship.
The picnic has dissolved, sending suitor
and sought home, to separate beds.
The waves of the Agi swell like a book left out,
blurred ink of words he would have read to her, to say

This is my voice, my mouth, my face at the gate.

Bamboo and Poppies

Where gold's effaced, golden light breaks in,

lending the poppies a royal protection. Bamboo

leans against girls sweet and pent

as virgins. At their lives' opening, a green

father ushered them. At the closing, a selfsame

husband. Their story is one of

captivity, or love: the coin's flipside. The gilt sky

is a mirror. Roots are fear, ignorance, loyalty . . .

Maples

What is looked at too long
reddens: blush of attention. Blood-kissed,
audacious as sin. Trees do this,
attracting a harder gaze. How the eye
will wander down the maple's pretty body.
Rarest in nature, that shade.
As a sudden confession in bed, death
or marriage. Is there a prettier word
than *privacy*? Alone with ink, a notebook of
green observations, red feelings.

Swallows and Waves

Massive, the sea sweeps
and swerves, furious as a dragon.
Salt-hewn, foam-
roughed, it troubles the thirteen
swallows who cluster—
identical, overlapping—trying
to build one steady thing.
Mist wets their breasts
and makes flying heavy. The sea
has no shore. All middle,
dense as middle age.
Birds may be welcome, then,
as minor miracles, granting grace
to that universal struggle.

Young Samurai on Horseback

Astride the downcast, tasseled animal, the soldier

is somber. His horse twists, impatient.

Two women within the house,

whispering behind a pane, reinforce

a solitary mood.

Adrenaline mixes with caution, ready

to ride toward what is destined. What molten gold

feels before it's poured into the ring mold.

The Love Letter

Bathed in gold, the mother and her
miniature arc together,
as in disaster, diamonds and fish
on cloth suffused into chaos.
Shared faraway look
of poignant longing, toward
the writ confession. Dissonance
of reading a lover's ink, left bodiless.

Descending Geese at Katada

As flown from orange sunset, over mountain-
shaded sea, at eventide. As boats
are drawn in, sails begin to undress, or arrive anxious,
fully bare-masted. Fishermen navigate reeds
that signal *harbor,*
and the homecoming emotions enlarge.
Water holds blueness not much longer. Death
will costume it in its color, and the honking of geese
will give voice to the grieving.

Horses Romping on the Beach

Gold for cloud, for shore. Leafed
clouds cushion the beach where wind bends
twin trees, the minutes-
older one looking ever after its brother.
Eight horses—pinto and chestnut, gray
and ink—frolic. Array of flank and teeth,
they play: excitable bodies.
In a depthless present, their drinking,
wrestling, nuzzling highlights the human
absence. Gold dust
inside bamboo, the penetrating night. Iron
the horses, drawn to the eye's magnet.

The Poet Li Po Admiring a Waterfall

Vast scroll of endless blue

images, the elastic body in contrast

with the crag and skeleton

of brush, the crescent moon of

the poet before it,

come to shred last petty

thoughts, a man looking long

at an *unthinking*, *unfeeling*, soon him-

self without mind, without art.

Carp Lured by Fallen Cherry Blossom Petals

From under greasy banks made of mud and sickly
weeds and history, the muscular one (shunned, condemned)
is drawn into the current's event—comic mouth agog,
puny mustache twitching—as the pale
pinks roil in the upstream, their newness limp with fallenness
(suicidal girls), veined heartbreak, and he's the one,
the only one who sees them, now toward, now past him.

Woman Tearing a Love Letter

Doors slid open, she takes in the physical world,

where she has not lived. The fantasy

must end. Teeth rip those recollections, promises,

fragments

already at her feet. Ink's perfume

has soured. Peonies, neglected, shrink: death

at the edges. The worm's found its route. The pout

of lust turns to grimace. This, this is the present.

Butterflies

The hole at the center

of the galaxy is a black butterfly,

large and dominant, off-kilter.

From her, others emerge,

encircling her at birth, tethered

forever to the spoke

and word of her, bleak

headache and blindfold of her,

well and will of her.

Their essence is shame, air

trellis a prison, sorrow and vaster

visiting every flower, no reason

to be but to wreathe her.

The Insistent Lover

As the blind worm thrashes in sunlight

when dirty covers are removed. In pain but

pleading for more. Drunk

on love-talk, unembarrassed, indiscreet,

he tugs at her leaving.

In an unhandsome life, chooses extravagance

of flesh over allegiance to pride,

which does not ask and does not provide.

Golden Pheasant and Peonies

Deep dark gold of persimmon or Autumn

or permission withheld, he's

locked off as a vault while the peonies are ladies

at a bathhouse—exposed, etched

in driven white. Fragrant, sodden clouds

in Summer heat.

Noble, afraid, he wants to be found. Some sign

of *We are the same, in the deep dark down.*

Courtesan with Her Attendant

To be pleasing is an art. The apprentice steps into her charisma
as after a blizzard, following a mother, in snow's left-behind hollows.
As imitation bends toward knowledge, so pleasure
becomes a version of love.
When the lantern's lit, carried by
a stranger, then extinguished, and that man disrobes in her presence,
she must become the blown wick, made strong from experience.

Crickets, Cage, and Flowers

Like a prince, lonely in his palace,

the pet is kept. For luck, in

lacquered bondage.

Though indigo, orange, and red

the blossoms, their dulled silhouettes

behind the cage's bars

are ominous. Ah, how life light

at birth darkens at the end.

A cricket on the pampas grass

outside wants in. Plotting its escape

from what looks like freedom.

Firefly-Catching

From the cracked black sky come
Summer's pleasure-pulses. The mother drops one
into a hand-sized box, brought for this
purpose: revel before release. Her daughter,
strange and familiar, is the picture
of original experience, when excitement dominated veins
before slowing to a swollen flicker. Reminiscence
of girlhood before the lit-up river.

Bullock with Puppy

Haunch and shoulder, curvèd hoof and complacent
expression, ripple where flesh meets rope: become mountain.
Become the peace implicit in hugeness.
A queer pair, this land and its inhabitant, the puppy
so young, trustful of forces it feels are permanent,
certain as rivers and volcanos, as *home*, until they are gone.

Crows

In perpetual silhouette
perform against bronze. As exhausted
dancers, undressed behind
a scrim, the suggestion of nakedness
more erotic than . . .
En masse, they argue and flee
between slim sessions of peace. This
is existence: pain leashed
or unleashed.
Wings press against ribs in politesse
or unfurl in demonstrations
of power. When it's over,
crows remain as debris, Ebony confetti,
wrecking more the wrecked world.

Beauty with Cat

Marooned on an island of *unrequited,* of ache

without act. Castrated, the beast wearies

of preening. What between them will first capitulate?

His anger, her pity. In a panic,

he rises on hind legs, nearly a man, giving up

his confession, clawing her hem.

The reward for his tantrum is attention, how-

ever brief. Her smile is a conqueror's—softly mean,

secure—one accepting flowers from a girl.

Irises and Grasshopper

Client in a house of courtesans, tableau
of masculine and feminine.
The irises lie back, languorous, dark pink
at the centers and lighter at limbs.
The grasshopper, in his armor, grips the green
blade. Proximity is ecstasy
enough. A homesick soldier will kneel
at any woman's bed, to lose his mind beside
the strangeness of corolla and calyx.

Girl with Ox

The sinews of the ox's body, the muscles,

betray the limits of its independence.

Opium-white and residue-black, it balances the heavy

baskets to please its mistress.

Kneeling like a child for a punishment, or

a poem before the poet, it cannot act. The girl

commands it forward with a backward glance, anxious

as a mother or a poet in the aftermath.

The Bow Moon

The sun-bleached boat of it rests in the passivity
of sky. Moored between mountains
in the valley. Water that cascades in Spring is frozen mid-
skip. Silent. A footbridge
stretched like a spider web between trinkets
is empty. Travelers are home,
eating or sleeping. How exhausting to be a symbol
of safety and beauty, without twin or lover
or any likeness. It changes to please itself. This twilight
abandoned sculpture, stark in sapphire harbor.

Owl

The owl all softness,

exhaustion, high on the dead

tree, leafless limbs

stupefied, amputated of use,

save this seat.

Gray-washed, sated, harmless,

the owl will not kill,

though it peers excitedly

at ivy, little bloody foot-

prints of ivy

that resemble a familiar trail

of hurt, dragging through snow

a life's last moments.

Rabbits and Crows in the Night Snow

Disbelief of snow, suspended. So sudden
the plum blossoms
cannot close and hang instead
like broken parasols. As the heart, un-steeled
against pain, is broken.
How one rabbit leaps through terrible
darkness toward he who climbed the plum
tree, magically. Night–
coated crows home equally to each other,
like to like. Harmony,
though the field is deadly. Tonight it is fled
and life triumphs over tragedy.

Rabbits in Grass under the Moon

The pair turned transparent
as onion in oil, leached of characteristics
by the moon's pearlescent
power, washing even their shadows
as a mother scatters salt
on ink-marred cloth, restoring it.
Grass will break its own neck
to make their bed. The moon, she goes
thirsty sending light to drink.

Willow and Egret

When the egret releases its whiteness
and lifts, careless, against the willow, black
bill piercing the future, likewise
leggings dragging the past . . .
When the thousand-leafed tree sways
like nostalgia, curtains in a house
one is forever departing,
concentrate on the tranquility of solitude
and not its twin that is loneliness.
Wingèd moon over stilled ropes of green,
rising from seen to unseen.

Long-Tailed Blue Bird Flying over Azalea Blossoms

Its great tail is a burden, no accomplishment

at all. Therefore it wavers, casts off praise to progress

against the sea-buffed currents. A question of

confidence undermines wings' power,

which urges the body over the water's jagged surface,

above neck-breaking, crystalline shallows

so tempting to humans, who come here in distress,

looking out where the birds travel and down the cliff

where the pink and red azaleas try to live.

Mountain and River on the Kiso Road

The weasel in its Winter fur lies down

to dream. The silent film

freezes. Snow shuddering from shoulders,

the animal looks asleep.

Now landscape is deadened,

unblemished by fantasy.

Ice in the blue insistence

has no emotion. How glorious

its absence, the blankness of snowflakes

when they hit, unheard hiss of *is, is, is* . . .

Mandarin Ducks and Snow-Covered Reeds

When one dives, separate from her mate,

death is mere illusion.

She peers through water, assuring this.

When the crippled reeds rehabilitate, begin

their constant arc toward Spring,

pain seems impossible. So distance. So change-

of-heart. From above or beneath, how

a body will twist, intuiting fear

and replacing it with here-ness, exhibit of

faithfulness. Wordlessly saying *Be not afraid,*

Beloved, for the present exalts us!

Monkey and Wasp

In a column of near-
nothing, the monkey sits
in wonder, head tipped
back, as a child's often is.
Above him, a wasp spins—
obscure, beyond reach—
toy of flight, sting,
delighting the monkey's
almost-human eyes.
A limp fist betrays a wish
to catch and keep another,
to soothe those cries
in his palm's dry cradle.

Cranes and Pines

The pride of a father as his mate

and offspring eat never lessens. Though

cold can wreck a family, they are

alive, together. His black head and tail

feathers dense against the rest of him, the ice,

his kin, the horizon. What is visible—

those parts, the pine-tops in the distance—

is what Winter cannot conquer.

A child brought into the world invites

self-erasure. But slowly, slow

as the white body of the Empress reclining

in her chamber at night, whose beauty

is dying. On a feather bed, she's the goddess

of pine-scent, of snow. All of it hers,

the cranes and the cranes' hunger.

Blossoming Plum in Mist and in Snow

Silver and cold, the mist and snow are one

condition, one emotion: supreme safety wed to barest

devastation. *Shh*

whispers the abyss. Too new buds shiver

against it. A silver sun induces

a second sleep, to save them. When they wake, it will be

true Spring, blossoms forgiving as morning.

South Wind at Clear Dawn

Populace of pines huddled at Fuji's base: green

climbers who failed to summit. They are blameless, cannot

abide the coldness, the strictness of its face.

Wind must go alone and touch it anyway. Must swarm

the virgin snow into a bridal veil

worn against the superficial crowd below,

which is entertained by pain. While wind, stiff and untouchable

as a wife at her husband's funeral, feels everything.

Lovers in the Snow

With him drenched in ink and she
in its absence, existing within a sphere
of stillness: love letters unfolded
on pillows. Sensuous
admissions, the wilderness
of another breached, known.
More intimate if underfoot snow was
a mattress? They couldn't be closer.

Peach Blossom Spring

Thaw has turned the mountains a becoming blue, built

consequential lakes, making for the swan-lovers a place to neck

and gaze. Pavilions will fill

with friendships stoked all winter, one sentence laid

on another, slow smolder. When there are no more words

to burn, the mountains step out of snowy clothes,

giving example of how to be seen with new eyes. The fire dies,

is reborn with the strength of a thousand candle lights.

Young Man with Hawk

Talons latched onto her minder's wrist, the hawk
has picked a companion. Seduced
by the green of the hillside, the new-shoot Spring of cloth
draped over an arm, but mostly by being whistled
to and summoned. The pair stare up
where two hawks ride inside a pillar of sky. Choosing
one life means forsaking all others, though the young ones
do not yet feel the axe of this, in their happiness.

Two Beauties Leading a Horse

Up the fog-robed mountain they climb, bright.
kimonos as guides. In this element, the fog-
colored animal between them is irrelevant. Broad topics
narrow, with no men, no children
listening. Lightheaded as actresses taking off
make-up, they speak as themselves, exhale as clouds
confessions, thoughts undressed, a nakedness . . .

Grasshopper and Gourd Vine

Jungle of vine, trumpet. Hourglass gourds

jangling coins like warmongers.

A soldier bends in the preamble green

before leaping to his destiny. Swords crossed,

he allows no look back. The future,

tangled with conflict, fought-through

unknowns, must be broached lightly, alone.

Deer and Poems

Without fear, the herd gathers
in gold and silver, doe and buck
together at peaceable rest. The males'
new antlers stroke the lake
as they drink. Cask of hope broken
open, relief floods the scene.
To the brushed surface they bow,
honoring their living
and honoring the dead, ephemeral
now as poems hung in loose
calligraphy, in an empty place that feels
no wind. Which is Eternity.

Boy Dancing with a Hobby-Horse

Drum cast down, windmill untouched, he flexes

preference, dances with the horse-

head hoisted high above his own. Delighted

against a camouflage of like-minded flowers, the yellows

and greens work to keep him hidden,

safe in imagination, before the world gallops in, offering

promises of glory, real swords and real horses.

Chrysanthemums at Night

The strength almost ugly in daylight goes slack

in the dark. Tendrils, unkempt, sway. Heavy heads

empty. Leaves unpin. New mothers remember

lovers, limber poses used then. Still young,

they smoke outside, unseen by husbands, feeling wild

animal eyes, near and indifferent. Irrational dis-

obedience must stay restrained. A lover's face lingers.

Into smoke goes his name, his name, his name.

The Kegon Falls

Water-tumbler, breaking its back
against cliffs that guide the appointed death-
route. It rises whitely,
wraithlike, before dying entire. All
of life—rains, roe twitching
into swimmers, mud's strangulations,
ache of sun like oppressive love—crashes
up. First freedom, first triumph.

Three Women under a Flowering Cherry Tree

Courtesans in sumptuous kimonos, whose patterns—

lithe branches, rabbits—overlap

in violets, peaches, greens. Collusion of newborn colors

against the complex texture of

exited bedcovers. What is said stays secret,

in the primacy of Spring's brief flowering. Eye and spirit,

friendship, refresh here, in this the pleasure district.

Bullfinch on a Branch of Weeping Cherry

Returned like a young man from the comfort

of a courtesan. The damp breast thumps on this first

warm morning, when sunlight heats the dew

but lets it glisten. Sole client

among clusters of beauties, left to choose. Feeling

desirable. How an eye flits through those clouds. Able to

see clearly the blue dawn. No need for song.

A Mother Dressing Her Son in a Kimono

He stands, suddenly more man than animal,

but naked and bald-headed, his penis a bashful sprig.

Spring has delivered its news. She kneels

and guides sleeves over fresh muscles. Her breasts

retreat back to ornament. The romance of their first

year together, milky nights in bed, quietly ends.

Lotus and Willow in Moonlight

The full moon casts its wealth

to Earth, spilling gold onto the lotus pond, the horizon.

A lotus blossom, which has known

the poverty of loneliness, is now free to express.

Lit on Nature's stage, in a Noh dance,

it forges emotions of pity and strength—

ghost among the living.

A green chorus accompanies its whiteness,

underscoring the plaintive story.

Ivory beauty, plaiting the pond with its silent song,

as a comb ornaments a woman's hair.

Sources

The artworks referenced in this collection were viewed in the following sources:

The Flowering of Edo Period Painting: Japanese Masterworks from the Feinberg Collection. Exhibition catalogue. The Metropolitan Museum of Art, New York, 2014. Print.

> *Blossoming Plum in Mist and in Snow*, Matsumura Goshun, 1752–1811
> *Carp Lured by Fallen Cherry Blossom Petals*, Katsu Jagyoku, 1732–1778
> *Chrysanthemums at Night*, Itō Jakuchū, 1716–1800
> *Peach Blossom Spring*, Watanabe Gentai, 1749–1822
> *Woman Tearing a Love Letter*, Katsukawa Shunshō, 1726–1792

Hartley, Craig, and Celia R. Withycombe. *Prints of the Floating World: Japanese Woodcuts from the Fitzwilliam Museum, Cambridge*. Cambridge: Fitzwilliam Museum in Association with Lund Humphries, London, 1997. Print.

> *Irises and Grasshopper*, Katsushika Hokusai, 1760–1849
> *Lover Taking Leave of a Courtesan*, Suzuki Harunobu, 1724–1770
> *A Mother Dressing Her Son in a Kimono*, Suzuki Harunobu
> *Mountain and River on the Kiso Road*, Utagawa Hiroshige, 1797–1858

Hillier, J. *Japanese Colour Prints*. Oxford: Phaidon, 1981. Print.

> *The Bow Moon*, Utagawa Hiroshige
> *Boy Dancing with a Hobby-Horse*, Ishikawa Toyonobu, 1711–1785
> *Firefly-Catching*, Eishōsai Chōki, 1756–1808
> *Golden Pheasant and Peonies*, Isoda Koryūsai, 1735–1790
> *The Insistent Lover*, Sugimura Jihei, active c. 1681–1703

The Love Letter, Okumura Masanobu, 1683–1764

Illing, Richard. *The Art of Japanese Prints*. London: Octopus, 1980. Print.

Sparrows and Camellia, Keisai Eisen, 1790–1848

Japan Is the Key . . . Carnegie Museum of Art, Pittsburgh. 2013.
Descending Geese at Katada, Utagawa Hiroshige
An Eagle Attacking a Monkey under a Pine Tree, Isoda Koryūsai
Hairdresser, Kitagawa Utamaro, 1753–1806
South Wind at Clear Dawn, Katsushika Hokusai
Three Women under a Flowering Cherry Tree, Chōkōsai Eishō,
    active c. 1780-1800
*Two Women, One Seated on a Bench Smoking a Pipe and Another Holding a Fan,
    under the Light of the Crescent Moon*, Isoda Koryūsai
*A Woman Coming from under the Mosquito Netting and Lighting Her Pipe at the
    Wick of a Lantern*, Utagawa Kunisada, 1786–1865

Michener, James A. *Japanese Prints: From the Early Masters to the Modern*. Tokyo: C.E. Tuttle, 1959. Print.
Girl Playing Samisen, Unknown
Girl with Ox, Suzuki Harunobu
Lovers in the Snow, Suzuki Harunobu
The Poet Li Po Admiring a Waterfall, Katsushika Hokusai
Young Man with Hawk, Isoda Koryūsai
Young Samurai on Horseback, Okumura Masanobu

Stern, Harold P. *Birds, Beasts, Blossoms, and Bugs: The Nature of Japan*. New York: H.N. Abrams, 1976. Print.
Bamboo and Poppies, Kanō Shigenobu, active c. 1620–1640
Bullock with Puppy, Nagasawa Rosetsu, 1747–1799
Cranes and Pines, Soga Shōhaku, 1730–1781

Crickets, Cage, and Flowers, Shibata Zeshin, 1807–1891

Crows, Unknown

Deer and Poems, Tawaraya Sōtatsu, active c. 1600-1643

Grasshopper and Gourd Vine, Shibata Zeshin

Horses Romping on the Beach, Unknown

Lotus and Willow in Moonlight, Tsubaki Chinzan, 1801–1854

Mandarin Ducks and Snow-Covered Reeds, Itō Jakuchū

Maples, Suzuki Kiitsu, 1796–1858

Monkey and Wasp, Mori Sosen, 1747–1821

Owl, Watanabe Shikō, 1683–1755

Peacock, Nagasawa Rosetsu

Rabbits and Crows in the Night Snow, Dagyoku Sanjin, 1733–1778

Rooster and Hen before Hydrangeas, Itō Jakuchu

Swallows and Waves, Okamoto Shūki, 1807=1862

Tiger and Dragon, Unkoku Tōgan, 1547–1618

Tiger Licking Its Leg, Komai Genki, 1747–1797

Willow and Egret, Suzuki Kiitsu

Tokyo National Museum, Tokyo. 2014.

Beauty with Cat, Isoda Koryūsai

Butterflies, Kubo Shunman, 1757-1820

Two Beauties Leading a Horse, Yamazaki Ryūjo, active c. 1716-1736

White, Julia M., Reiko Mochinaga Brandon, and Yoko Woodson. *Hokusai and Hiroshige: Great Japanese Prints from the James A. Michener Collection, Honolulu Academy of Arts.* San Francisco: Asian Art Museum of San Francisco in Association with the Honolulu Academy of Arts and U of Washington, Seattle and London, 1998. Print.

Hibiscus and Korean Nightingale, Utagawa Hiroshige

Long-Tailed Blue Bird Flying over Azalea Blossoms, Utagawa Hiroshige

Rabbits in Grass under the Moon, Dagyoku Sanjin

Whitford, Cecilia. *Japanese Prints*. London: Thames and Hudson, 1977. Print.

Bullfinch on a Branch of Weeping Cherry, Katsushika Hokusai

Courtesan with Her Attendant, Suzuki Harunobu

The Kegon Falls, Keisai Eisen

Riverboat Party, Hishikawa Moronobu, 1618-1694

Sudden Rain on Mt. Tempō, Yashima Gakutei, 1786-1868

Acknowledgments

Grateful acknowledgment is given to the editors of the publications in which these poems first appeared:

Australian Book Review: "Descending Geese at Katada"

Boston Review: "Girl with Ox"

The Buenos Aires Review: "Firefly-Catching," "Golden Pheasant and Peonies," "Irises and Grasshopper," "Mountain and River on the Kiso Road" (with Spanish translation)

The Cincinnati Review: "Bamboo and Poppies," "Maples," "Tiger and Dragon"

Harvard Divinity Bulletin: "The Kegon Falls," "A Mother Dressing Her Son in a Kimono"

Iron Horse Literary Review: "The Bow Moon," "Boy Dancing with a Hobby-Horse"

Kyoto Journal: "Cranes and Pines"

The Nation: "Crows"

New Letters: "Sudden Rain on Mt. Tempō"

The New Republic: "Hairdresser"

Orion: "Mandarin Ducks and Snow-Covered Reeds"

Poetry International: "Two Women, One Seated on a Bench Smoking a Pipe and Another Holding a Fan, under the Light of the Crescent Moon"

Poetry Kanto: "Deer and Poems," "Monkey and Wasp," "Owl," "Tiger Licking Its Leg"

Poetry New Zealand: "Girl Playing Samisen," "Young Man with Hawk"

Psychology Tomorrow Magazine: "Courtesan with Her Attendant"

Stand: "Lover Taking Leave of a Courtesan," "Sparrows and Camellia"

Subtropics: "A Woman Coming from under the Mosquito Netting and Lighting Her Pipe at the Wick of a Lantern," "Long-Tailed Blue Bird Flying over Azalea Blossoms"

Tricycle: "Crickets, Cage, and Flowers," "Lotus and Willow in Moonlight," "Rabbits and Crows in the Night Snow," "Rooster and Hen before Hydrangeas," "Swallows and Waves," "Willow and Egret"

"Girl with Ox" appeared on *Poetry Daily* in 2015.

PAULA BOHINCE is the author of two previous collections, both from Sarabande: *The Children* and *Incident at the Edge of Bayonet Woods*. Her poems have appeared in *The New Yorker, The New York Review of Books, Poetry, Granta, The TLS, The Irish Times, Australian Book Review,* and elsewhere. She has received prizes from the Poetry Society of America and the UK National Poetry Competition, as well as the "Discovery"/*The Nation* Award. She has been the Amy Lowell Poetry Travelling Scholar, the Dartmouth Poet in Residence at The Frost Place, a Fellow of the National Endowment for the Arts, and a Hawthornden Fellow, among other honors. She lives in Pennsylvania.

Sarabande Books is a nonprofit literary press located in Louisville, KY, and Brooklyn, NY. Founded in 1994 to champion poetry, short fiction, and essay, we are committed to creating lasting editions that honor exceptional writing. For more information, please visit sarabandebooks.org.